ENDANGERED WILDLIFE

Milton McClaren

Bob Samples

CONSULTANT

Bill Hammond

Ginn Publishing Canada Inc.

CONNECTIONS: THE LIVING PLANET
Endangered Wildlife

DEVELOPMENTAL EDITOR
Jenifer A. Ludbrook

EDITORS
Sharon Stewart
Anne MacInnes

DESIGN
Word & Image Design Studio

ILLUSTRATORS
Susanna Denti: 6–7, 9, 11 (motif),
    17–19, 26–27, 36, 46, 47, 48
Pierre Fortin: 28–29
Suzanne Gauthier: 4, 10
Barbara Gibson: 20–21
Susan Leopold: 34
Bo-Kim Louie: 12–15

C90010
ISBN 0-7702-2005-3

ABCDEFGHI   2000 99876543

ACKNOWLEDGMENTS

"Once There Were No Pandas." Reprinted by permission of Dutton Children's Books, a division of Penguin Books, U.S.A., Inc., from ONCE THERE WERE NO PANDAS by Margaret Greaves, © 1985 by Margaret Greaves.
"Our Endangered Wildlife." Reprinted by permission, National Geographic WORLD. Copyright 1990 National Geographic Society.
"Nature Made You, Manatee" by Norma Farber. Copyright © 1991 Miriam Farber.
Painting of a passenger pigeon by John James Audubon courtesy of The Audubon Society.
"The Dolphin" by Mary Ann Coleman. First published in CRICKET magazine and to appear in THE DREAMS OF HUMMINGBIRDS: POEMS FROM NATURE by Albert Whitman & Company in 1993. Reprinted by permission of the author.
"Little Orphan Ape." Text and photos by Evelyn Gallardo. Reprinted by kind permission of the author.
"Meet Dr. Galdikas." Reprinted from the August 1990 issue of RANGER RICK magazine with the permission of the publisher, the National Wildlife Federation. Copyright © 1990 by NWF.
"Flying High." Reprinted from OWL Magazine with permission of the publisher, The Young Naturalist Foundation.

PHOTOGRAPHS

Cover: (front) Gary Milburn/Tom Stack & Associates, (back) BIOS (Compost/Visage)/Peter Arnold Inc.; 1: (top) James H. Carmichael, Jr., (second from top) Kevin Schafer, (second from bottom) Kevin Schafer, (bottom) Michael & Patricia Fogden; 2: HOA-Qui Pavard/Publiphoto; 3: (top left) James H. Carmichael, Jr., (top right) M. Austerman/Animals, Animals, (bottom left) Kim Heacox/DRK Photo, (bottom right) Erwin & Peggy Bauer; 4–5: (top left) Mickey Gibson/Animals, Animals, (top centre) James H. Carmichael, Jr., (top right) Michael Dick/Animals, Animals, (bottom left) Michael & Patricia Fogden, (bottom right) Robert & Linda Mitchell, (background) Lynn Stone/Earth Scenes; 6: Randall Hyman; 8: Martha Hill/Kevin Schafer; 9: Michael & Patricia Fogden; 11: Logo courtesy of World Wildlife Fund, (bottom right) John Cancalosi/DRK Photo; 16: Kevin Schafer; 17: Kathy Watkins/Images of Nature; 18: T. Kitchin/Tom Stack & Associates; 19: (left) Laura Riley/Bruce Coleman Inc., (centre) Jeff Foott, (right) Courtney Milne/Comstock; 22: Wayne Lynch/DRK Photo; 23: Carson Baldwin, Jr./Earth Scenes; 24: Fred Bavendam/Peter Arnold Inc.; 25: Fred Bavendam/Peter Arnold Inc.; 26: Fred Bavendam/Peter Arnold Inc.; 30: Kevin Schafer; 31: Randall Hyman; 32: (left) D. Vayer/Publiphoto, (right) Bruce Coleman Inc.; 33: Zig Leszczynski/Animals, Animals, 35: (left) Gerry Ellis/The Wildlife Collection, (right) Randall Hyman; 36–41: Evelyn Gallardo; 42: BIOS (Compost/Visage)/Peter Arnold Inc.; 43: Jeff Foott; 44: (top) Stephen J. Krasemann/Peter Arnold Inc., (bottom) OWL Magazine; 45: (top) Karen Magnuson Beil/OWL Magazine, (bottom) Robert P. Carr/Bruce Coleman Inc.; 46: John Cancalosi/DRK Photo.

Every reasonable precaution has been taken to trace the owners of copyrighted material and to make due acknowledgment. Any omission will be gladly rectified in future editions.

CONTENTS

Introduction   4

World of the Endangered 6

What is an endangered species?   8

Going, Going, Gone 9
Activity: What Is Wildlife? 10
China's Furry National Treasure 11
Once There Were No Pandas 12

Threats to wild species   16

Our Endangered Wildlife 17
Activity: Why Wildlife Disappears:
    The Spotted Owl 22
Special Report: The Chestnut Challenge 23
Vanishing Manatees 24
Nature Made You, Manatee 25
Issue: Furbish's Lousewort—For and Against 26
Why Protect Species? 28
Activity: Now That You're Gone 30

Working to save wildlife   31

Wildlife in Captivity 32
Special Report: Back from the Brink:
    The Story of the Oryx 33
The Dolphin.......................................34
Activity: Do Zoos Help Save Wildlife? 35
Little Orphan Ape 36
Meet Dr. Galdikas! 42
Special Report: The Call of the Cranes 43
Activity: Saving Endangered Wildlife 44

What *You* Can Do 46
A Flock of Activities 47
Endangered Wildlife Word List 48

INTRODUCTION

"**E**xtinction is forever. Endangered means it's not too late!"

Will people of the future ever forgive us for causing so many extinctions?

More plants and animals are becoming extinct today than at any time since the last days of the dinosaurs!

Will there be any rainforests or herds of wild animals left for our children to see?

If all the beasts were gone, people would die from great loneliness of spirit.

World of the Endangered

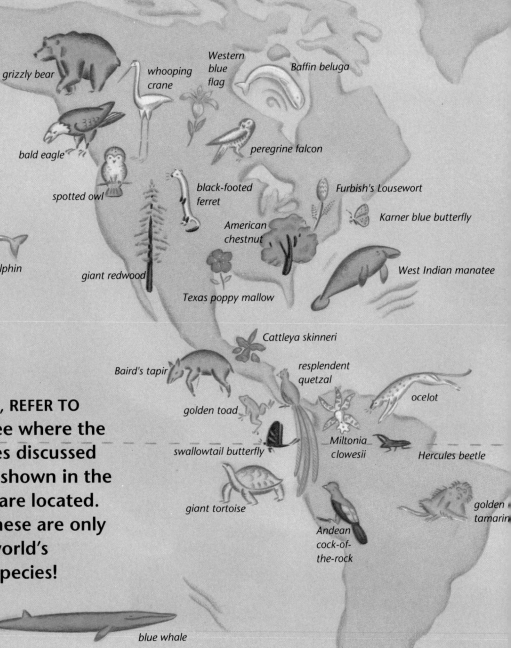

grizzly bear

whooping crane

Western blue flag

Baffin beluga

bald eagle

peregrine falcon

spotted owl

black-footed ferret

Furbish's Lousewort

Karner blue butterfly

American chestnut

dolphin

giant redwood

West Indian manatee

Texas poppy mallow

Cattleya skinneri

Baird's tapir

resplendent quetzal

ocelot

golden toad

swallowtail butterfly

Miltonia clowesii

Hercules beetle

giant tortoise

golden tamarin

Andean cock-of-the-rock

blue whale

AS YOU READ, REFER TO this map to see where the wildlife species discussed in the text or shown in the photographs are located. Remember, these are only a *few* of the world's endangered species!

WHAT IS AN ENDANGERED SPECIES?

The words "endangered species" and "endangered wildlife" pop up in newspaper headlines, television programs, magazine articles, and many, many books these days. But just what exactly does "endangered" mean? And what's a species, anyway?

Going, Going, Gone

Scientists use the word **species** to mean a group of plants or animals that is different in some way from all other groups. All the members of a species can breed with each other and produce the same kind of offspring. Only about 1 1/2 million species are known so far, but many scientists believe that there may be anywhere from 5 to 10 million species in the world. Others believe there may even be 30 million or more!

All over the world, wildlife species are dying out, or becoming **extinct**, faster than ever before in the history of the planet. And most of the extinctions going on today are directly caused by human beings. To keep track of what is happening to the world's wildlife, scientists use special words to describe which species are in the most danger of disappearing. The chart below shows what each word means and gives examples of species the word describes.

WORD	MEANING	EXAMPLES
extinct	a species that has no known survivors	tyrannosaurus rex passenger pigeon quagga
endangered	a species very likely to become extinct	rosy periwinkle panda bowhead whale
threatened	a species not yet in danger, but likely to be in the future	resplendent quetzal Western blue flag Nile crocodile
vulnerable	a species at risk because of its small numbers	polar bear giant redwood Hercules beetle

What Is Wildlife?

Does the word "wildlife" mean only species that have no contact with people? Or does it mean any species that doesn't depend on humans for food or shelter the way tame, or **domesticated**, species do? With some friends, discuss which of the following plants and animals are wildlife.

- birds at a feeder
- a seal in a marine park
- grass in a lawn
- a family dog
- dandelions in a lawn
- cows in a pasture
- a mosquito in your bedroom
- rabbits in a woodland
- shade trees planted along a street
- fungus on stale bread

Now check your backyard and your schoolyard for wildlife. List the animals and plants you find. (If you're not sure of the names of some of them, use an encyclopedia and books from the library to find out.)

Work as a group to write definitions of "wild" and "domesticated."

China's Furry National Treasure

Logo of the World Wildlife Fund

What's black and white, furry, and loaded with charm? A panda, of course. The oddest thing about pandas is their eating habits. Their main food is the arrow bamboo plant, and they must eat an incredible amount just to stay alive. An adult panda needs to eat ten to twenty kilograms of bamboo every day. That takes it about fourteen hours of steady chewing. It spends its spare time resting. No wonder!

Pandas used to live in large areas of southeast and southwest Asia, but today they are found only in the misty mountains of southwest China. Scientists believe that there are only about a thousand of them left. One reason for this is that poachers still hunt them for their skins. An even bigger problem is that many of the panda's home forests have been cleared for farmland. To make things worse, the arrow bamboo flowers and dies down every fifty to sixty years. When that happens, the pandas must switch to another type of bamboo until the arrow bamboo grows again. Some can do this, but others die of starvation.

China has declared its pandas a national treasure and has set aside twelve protected areas for them. There is also a panda research centre where Chinese and foreign scientists study these amazing animals. With a lot of help from their friends in China and all around the world, there is at least a chance that China's precious pandas will survive.

Once There Were No Pandas

A Chinese Legend

by Margaret Greaves

Long, long ago in China, when the earth and the stars were young, there were none of the black-and-white bears that the Chinese call xiong mao and that we call pandas. But deep in the bamboo forests lived bears with fur as white and soft and shining as new-fallen snow. The Chinese called them bai xiong, which means "white bear."

In a small house at the edge of the forest lived a peasant and his wife and their little daughter, Chien-min.

One very hot day, Chien-min was playing alone at the edge of the forest. The green shadow of the trees looked cool as water, and a patch of yellow buttercups shone invitingly.

"They are only *just* inside the forest," said the little girl to herself. "It will take only a minute to pick some."

She slipped in among the trees. But when she had picked her flowers, she looked around, puzzled. There were so many small paths! Which one led back to the village?

As she hesitated, something moved and rustled among the leaves nearby. She saw a delicate head with big ears, a slim body dappled with light and shadow. It was one of the small deer of the forest. Chien-min had startled it, and it bounded away between the trees. She tried

to follow, hoping it might lead her home. But almost at once it was out of sight, and Chien-min was completely lost.

She began to be frightened. But then she heard another sound—something whimpering not far away. She ran toward the place, forgetting her fear, wanting only to help.

There, close to a big thorny bush, squatted a very small white bear cub. Every now and then he shook one of his front paws and licked it, then whimpered again.

"Oh, you poor little one!" Chien-min ran over and knelt beside the little bear. "Don't cry! I'll help you. Let me see it."

The cub seemed to understand. He let her take hold of his paw. Between the pads was a very sharp thorn. Chien-min pinched it between her finger and thumb and very carefully drew it out. The cub rubbed his head against her hands as she stroked him.

A moment later a huge white bear came crashing through the trees, growling fiercely. But when she saw that the little girl was only playing with her cub, her anger vanished. She licked his paw, then nuzzled Chien-min as if she, too, were one of her cubs.

The mother bear was so gentle that the child took courage and put her arms round her neck, stroking the soft fur. "How beautiful you are!"

she said. "Oh, if only you could show me the way home."

At once the great bear ambled forward, grunting to the cub and his new friend to follow. Fearlessly now, Chien-min held on to the thick white coat and very soon found that she was at the edge of the forest again, close to her own home.

From that day on, she often went into the forest. Her parents were happy about it, knowing their daughter was safe under the protection of the great white bear. She met many of the other bears, too, and many of their young, but her special friend was always the little cub she had helped. She called him Niao Niao, which means "very soft," because his fur was so fine and beautiful.

The mother bear showed the little girl her secret home, a den in the hollow of a great tree. Chien-min went there many times, played with the cubs, and learned the ways of the forest. Always the great she-bear led her safely back before nightfall.

One warm spring afternoon, Chien-min was sitting by the hollow tree, watching the cubs at play, when she saw a stealthy movement between the bamboos. A wide, whiskered face. Fierce topaz eyes. Small tufted ears. A glimpse of spotted, silky fur.

Chien-min sprang up, shouting a warning. But she was too late. With bared teeth and lashing tail, the hungry leopard had leaped upon Niao Niao.

Chien-min forgot all fear in her love for her friend. Snatching up a great stone, she hurled it at the leopard. The savage beast dropped his prey but turned on her, snarling with fury. At the same moment, the she-bear charged through the trees like a thunderbolt.

The leopard backed off, terrified by her anger. But as he turned to run, he struck out at Chien-min with his huge claws, knocking her to the ground.

The bears ran to Chien-min, growling and whining and licking her face. But the little girl never moved. She had saved Niao Niao's life by the loss of her own.

News of her death swept through the forest. From miles away, north, south, east, and west, all the white bears gathered to mourn. They wept and whimpered for their lost friend, rubbing their paws in the dust of the earth and wiping the tears from their eyes. As they did so, the wet dust left great black smears across their faces. They beat their paws against their bodies in bitter lamentation, and the wet dust clung to their fur in wide black bands.

But although the bears sorrowed for Chien-min, and her parents and friends mourned her, they were all comforted to know that she was happy. Guan-yin, the beautiful Goddess of Mercy, would give her a special place in heaven, where her selfless love for her friend would always be rewarded.

And from that day to this, there have been no white bears, *bai xiong*, anywhere in China. Instead there are the great black-and-white bears, *xiong mao*, that we call pandas, still mourning for their lost friend, Chien-min.

THREATS TO WILD SPECIES

Why are certain plants and animals in danger of disappearing? To survive, all species need certain basic things. These needs are food, water, space to grow or live in, and the ability to have offspring. When any of these needs isn't met, a species is in trouble.

Our Endangered
Wildlife

Before this day ends, the last of some 45 kinds of plants and animals will die. A month from now, 1400 more species will be gone. Within a year, the number of vanished species will total about 17 500. Scientists provide these estimates, which represent the most hopeful case. The actual numbers may prove to be much higher.

Among the vanishing species are African elephants. Ivory hunters kill the elephants illegally at the rate of about 200 a day. Farmers in overcrowded countries squeeze elephant herds into spaces too small to support them. Ten years ago, 1 1/2 million elephants roamed the African countryside. Now perhaps 400 000 remain.

Loss of the elephant, nearly everyone agrees, would be tragic. Even worse, say scientists, would be the loss of smaller, often microscopic, species. "It's the tiny species that really run the planet," says Dr. Thomas Lovejoy, a **conservationist** with the Smithsonian Institution in Washington, D.C. "Bacteria make digestion possible. Fungi give us penicillin and other medicines. Grass and other plants contribute oxygen. 'Squirmies' such as worms and termites are nature's recyclers."

Huge numbers of *unknown* plants and animals are also in danger. The earth, according to various estimates, supports between 5 million and *80* million species. Of these, scientists have found and named only about 1 1/2 million. "Species," says Dr. Lovejoy, "are disappearing before we have a chance to learn how they might benefit the rest of the planet."

A SYMBOL NEARLY LOST

In 1782, when the eagle became the symbol of the United States, many thousands nested in all parts of North America. Some two hundred years later, only fifteen hundred pairs remained outside Alaska. The main reason: poisoning by DDT. With DDT banned in the U.S., the eagles, like the peregrine falcons, are slowly increasing in number.

▼

A CLOUDED FUTURE ▶

Clearing of Asian land for farms has destroyed much of the forest where clouded leopards once lived. Poaching— illegal hunting—adds to the cats' problems. Some leopards still survive in remote hideaways, but for how long?

Thousands of kinds of tropical plants could help feed a growing world population. About four out of every ten prescription medicines come from ingredients found in plants. Some animals also provide medicines.

"It's natural for species to become extinct over millions of years," says Dr. Lovejoy. "What's *un*natural is that humans are speeding up the process many times over."

People are doing this in four main ways: destroying wildlife **habitats**, overhunting, introducing new species that endanger **native** wildlife, and polluting the environment. These activities affect all species in one way or another. "All life is interconnected," cautions Dr. Lovejoy.

THE TOLL ON TORTOISES ▲

In the 1800s, sailors stopped at Ecuador's Galápagos Islands to stock up on food— giant tortoises. While the ships lay at anchor, cats and rats came ashore. They did more harm than the sailors. By eating eggs and hatchlings, the introduced animals gradually reduced the tortoise population from 250 000 to 15 000.

INNOCENT VICTIM ▶

Hunting almost wiped out the black-footed ferret. Yet the ferret was not the hunted animal; the prairie dog was. For centuries the two animals lived in the same burrow systems on the North American prairie. Prairie dogs ate grass, and ferrets ate prairie dogs. Then ranchers who needed the grass for cattle waged war on prairie dogs. The result: fewer prairie dogs and near-extinction for the ferrets.

19

Is there time to prevent disaster? Just barely, say scientists. They agree that these steps must be taken:

Control human population growth so that all living things do not have to compete so fiercely for resources. Experts say it took some seventeen hundred years for world population to double from three hundred million to six hundred million. Today's population will double in just eighty-two years.

Educate people worldwide about the dangers of failing to conserve. People must learn to make recycling a habit and to use the land wisely.

Save tropical forests through international action. Such forests cover only a fraction of the land but support at least half the world's species. The forests are critically endangered.

Worldwide action will be difficult and costly. But scientists agree that action must be taken—quickly. The clock is ticking....

FOUR THREATS TO WILDLIFE

OVERHUNTING ▶

Many people in Asia believe powdered rhino horn is powerful medicine. In parts of the Middle East, a dagger with a rhino-horn handle symbolizes power. Such traditions result in tremendous pressure to harvest more and more rhino horns. A single rhino horn brings a poacher as much as $1125. In some of the African countries where black rhinos live, that's what an average worker earns in two years. The profits are so high that black rhino hunting continues in spite of laws against it. The species is now endangered. Other animals endangered through overhunting include the blue whale, the cheetah, the grizzly bear, and the mountain gorilla.

◀ HABITAT LOSS

Most people have never heard of the Texas poppy mallow. This plant grows only in a few places in Texas, and only where there is a deep layer of sand. Now the mallow is in danger of disappearing. Construction companies that use sand for building have destroyed much of its habitat.

Wind and rain spread poisons across the land and through the oceans. Some poisons take years to do their damage. The peregrine falcon almost disappeared because of DDT, a pest-killing chemical sprayed from airplanes. Once in the environment, DDT remains a very long time. It enters the food chain and becomes more and more concentrated as larger animals eat smaller ones. It causes birds of prey to lay thin-shelled eggs that break when the parents sit on them. After the United States banned DDT in 1972, more peregrine chicks began hatching. Now, slowly, the birds are making a comeback.

INTRODUCTION OF NEW SPECIES ▲

When Europeans first saw the animals of Australia, they were astounded. The animals didn't look like those at home. Many were marsupials—pouched mammals—like the rabbit-eared bandicoot. Australian animals soon got some surprises—unpleasant ones—of their own. The settlers brought in new species that competed for food and living space. Continents away from any natural enemies, the newcomers quickly multiplied, upsetting the balance among native species. Foxes hunted and killed bandicoots for food. Rabbits took over bandicoot burrows. Now, in its native land, the bandicoot struggles to survive.

The plant faces an additional threat from ranchers who plow it under to plant grass for cattle. When a plant disappears, animals that depend on it directly for food or shelter also suffer. In turn, species that depend on such animals are affected. All life, scientists say, is interrelated.

ACTIVITY

Why Wildlife Disappears: The Spotted Owl

The spotted owl lives only in the old-growth forests of the Pacific coast of North America. It roosts and breeds and gets all its food and water in the forest. Here's the way the spotted owl's needs would look on a web.

Many of the Pacific coast forests are being cut down. Air and water pollution are also a problem in the spotted owl's range. What effects might these things have on it?

Now work with some friends to find out more about another endangered species. You could record your findings on a web. Which of the four threats mentioned in "Our Endangered Wildlife" are affecting the species you have chosen?

Use your web as part of a presentation on the species you have researched. You could:

- create a bulletin board display
- publish a book about your findings
- get together with others to hold an Endangered Species Fair, with displays, readings, and performances

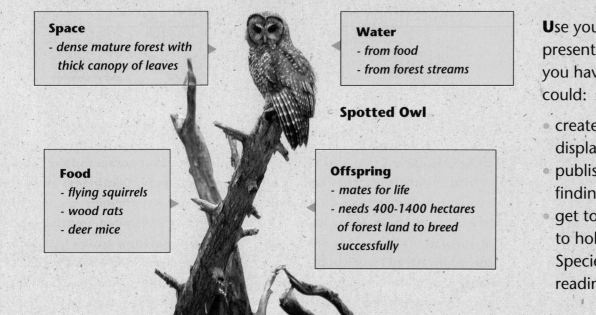

Space
- *dense mature forest with thick canopy of leaves*

Water
- *from food*
- *from forest streams*

Spotted Owl

Food
- *flying squirrels*
- *wood rats*
- *deer mice*

Offspring
- *mates for life*
- *needs 400-1400 hectares of forest land to breed successfully*

THE CHESTNUT CHALLENGE

A hundred years ago, millions of towering chestnut trees dotted the forests of eastern North America. These huge trees were a very valuable resource. The nuts were food for people and animals. People also used the ground-up bark to tan leather, and made fence posts and furniture out of its sturdy wood.

But in 1906, disaster struck. The chestnut trees around New York City started to die of a strange disease. What caused it? In 1904, some chestnut seedlings had been brought to New York from Asia. The seedlings carried tiny cells, called spores, that spread the disease. The spores were carried from tree to tree by the wind, and also by birds and insects. One woodpecker alone was found to have seven thousand spores on its feet!

Today, only a few American chestnut trees remain. Somehow they have survived the disease carried by the spores. And new trees still grow from the old roots of the fallen giants. They last a few years and some even produce nuts before the disease kills them.

Now scientists are working to cross the American chestnut tree with the Asian species, which somehow resists the disease. More help may come from Europe. There, scientists found that the deadly spores were killed off by another plant disease. Perhaps it can help save the American chestnut.

Meanwhile, people try to protect the last surviving American chestnut trees. As long as some are left, there's hope that we'll find an answer to the chestnut challenge.

Vanishing Manatees

Imagine an animal that looks like a giant Idaho potato with flippers! That's how one scientist describes the manatee, or sea cow. Like dolphins and whales, manatees are air-breathing mammals. They spend their entire lives in the water, and give birth to their young there.

The animal most North Americans know is the West Indian manatee. It summers along the Gulf coast and the southern Atlantic coast of the United States, and winters in the rivers and seas of Florida. West Indian manatees can grow to be more than three metres long, and weigh from 450 to 1350 kilograms. They are vegetarians, dining on water weeds and grasses. They're particularly fond of water hyacinths, a floating flower that often clogs Florida waterways.

Manatees may be too friendly and curious for their own good. In the past they were hunted for their meat, oil, and hides. Today, though, the main threat to them comes from the pollution and destruction of the waterways they depend on. Careless speedboaters are another danger. The slow-moving manatees often bask near the surface of rivers, and each year many are killed or wounded by the blades of propellers.

There are now only twelve hundred West Indian manatees left. The good news is that many people are trying to find ways to help them. Scientists are breeding them in captivity, and refuges have been created for them, where boats are not allowed. In other places, speed limits for boats are enforced. Today, people who do anything to hurt manatees can be fined or even sent to jail!

Nature Made You, **Manatee**

by Norma Farber

Nature made you, Manatee:

gave you life as fresh as ours,
bid you feed on river flowers,
gave you flippers, only two,
fore not aft, one pair too few,
gave you paddle for a tail,
made you mammal like a whale.

Mother Nature, she's the one
made you heavy as a ton,
gave you bristles on your nose,
no hind legs, nor even toes,
bid you wander lazily
up the stream and out to sea.

Nature loves you, Manatee!

FURBISH'S LOUSEWORT— FOR AND AGAINST

Save pandas! Save tigers! Save Furbish's Lousewort! Wait a minute, what's *that?* Furbish's Lousewort is an endangered plant that grows only along the St. John River in New Brunswick and Maine. Scientists believe that there are no more than five thousand of these plants left. Now there are plans to build a dam on the river. If the dam is built, all the places Furbish's Lousewort grows will be flooded, and the plant will become extinct.

Should Furbish's Lousewort be saved?

YES: I think we have to save this plant. Human beings have no right to wipe out any other species. I'm working with a conservation group to make sure that dam never gets built!

NO: You've got to be kidding! I live near the St. John River, and someday my town will need the electricity that dam will produce. I think people are more important than plants. Hey, don't get me wrong. I think we should do everything we can to save important species like elephants and pandas. But Furbish's Lousewort? Who cares?

YES: It's easy to get excited over cute, cuddly species like pandas, or glamorous ones like tigers or elephants. Most people don't care about plants the way they do about animals anyway. And it's easy to preach about saving species in other people's countries. I think we have a duty to save our own wildlife. Just because Furbish's Lousewort isn't a glamorous species is no reason to wipe it out.

 NO: I'm a construction worker. I've been out of work for two years, and building that dam will give me a job. I don't like to harm anything in the environment, but I have to put my family's needs first. Anyway, why can't they just **transplant** the lousewort to another location? Or plant seeds or something?

YES: It's not so easy to transplant wild plants or to get them to grow from seeds in a new location. If Furbish's Lousewort grows only in that one location, maybe that's the only place it *can* grow. And here's another thing to think about. Lousewort contains powerful chemicals that kill insects. Someday we might need just the combination of chemicals that this plant produces. What if it has become extinct?

NO: Saving endangered species sounds great. But extinction is a natural process. Why should we try to save every single species that's in danger? If there are so few Furbish's Lousewort plants left, maybe that means it's just not a successful species.

YES: I think it's okay for a species to become extinct naturally. But flooding the river valley where the lousewort grows isn't natural extinction. We have to stop wiping out species whenever it suits our needs!

NO: As long as more and more people are born on Earth, human needs are going to grow. And the more human needs grow, the more species are going to be endangered. I think we're going to have to make some tough choices about which species have to be protected and which don't. There are five hundred other kinds of lousewort in the world. I say Furbish's Lousewort isn't important enough to worry about.

What do you think?

Why Protect Species?

Do we really miss the dinosaurs? They became extinct millions of years ago, and the world seems to get along just fine without them. In fact, most of the species that once lived on our planet are now extinct. And if extinction is natural, why worry about endangered species?

One reason is that so *many* species are becoming endangered. Scientists believe that by the year 2000 there will be a million fewer species than there were a hundred years ago. Another reason is that just one species is to blame for a lot of the damage. That species is—us! If we're the ones causing the problem and also the only ones who can understand the problem and do something about it, shouldn't we at least try?

There are other reasons, too. The web of life is so complicated that we really can't predict just what will happen if a particular species disappears. All the species that depend on it for food, or shelter, or other needs, will be affected. And

all the species that depend on *them* will be, too. And so on and so on, just like ripples in a pond. This is especially true in **tropical rainforests**, where there are more species packed into the environment than anywhere else on Earth.

Another reason we should try to protect wild species is that we know how many valuable things have come from them in the past. Rubber, oils, and alcohol fuels are just a few examples. In fact, all of our food and most of our medicines have come from wild species, either directly or indirectly. A plant from Madagascar called the rosy periwinkle is now world-famous because it is used to make a

medicine that helps cure one type of cancer. That same plant is endangered today. What if it had become extinct years ago? Scientists are also discovering more wild food and plant species all the time. Who knows what we might miss if species become extinct? Maybe

Rosy periwinkle

something as important as wheat or rice, or as yummy as chocolate!

You may be thinking, well, we have enough food plants and lots of pigs and chickens now, so why do we have to worry about keeping wild species? The trouble is, our farm animals and crops need to be bred with wild members of the same species from time to time to make them stronger and healthier. Wild species are often important for pest control, too. If you need proof, just watch a ladybug gobble up the aphids on a rosebush!

The world of wild species is like a great big library crammed with books we don't know how to read yet. We haven't even discovered most of the species on Earth, and we don't fully understand the complicated information stored in the ones we do know about. It's not just that something we may need tomorrow may be stored in an endangered species. The real point is, what right do we have to destroy the richness of life on Earth? Don't forget, extinction is forever!

ACTIVITY

Now That You're Gone

Just 150 years ago, the most common bird in eastern North America was the passenger pigeon. There were millions of these birds. At migration time the sky could be darkened at midday by the numbers flying overhead. One writer talked of a flock taking three days to pass!

In 1914, the last passenger pigeon died at the Cincinnati zoo. The birds had been hunted for food and their habitat destroyed.

Find out more about the passenger pigeon, or about another animal or plant that has become extinct in the last five hundred years. Then say how you feel about it becoming extinct. You could:

- write a poem
- make a poster or mural
- give a talk
- pretend that you are the last of the species and write your life story

Painting of passenger pigeon by John James Audubon

WORKING TO SAVE WILDLIFE

Many scientists are very concerned about the worldwide extinctions of plants and animals. They have been speaking to world leaders to make sure they know about this problem. But is anything really being done to try to save endangered wildlife? Can the loss of plants and animals be stopped?

Wildlife in Captivity

Zoos and aquariums are in the news a lot lately. Some people believe they help save wildlife. That certainly wasn't true when zoos began! The first zoos were started over four thousand years ago. Ancient kings in Egypt and other lands collected wild animals and put them on display. The animals were caged and penned. Sometimes people were made to fight the fiercer animals, like lions and tigers.

Today's zoos are very different. The animals are well cared for. And although they're still behind fences, they often live in large fields or in jungle-like areas something like their natural habitats. Some people say that visitors to modern zoos know and care more about animals after seeing them live. This means they are more likely to help protect animals in the wild. But other people say it's cruel to take animals from their natural homes. Even when zoos cover large open areas, the animals are still captives. Zoo life is particularly hard for animals like chimpanzees that live in groups in the wild. Separated from their families and friends, they become lonely and bored. Some of them even become sick and die. The same is true of dolphins and killer whales, who live in large families and are used to the freedom of the open ocean.

Back from the Brink: The Story of the Oryx

Can an animal that has been born and raised in a zoo or captured years before be sent back to the wild and survive? The Arabian white oryx is an antelope with a white hide and two beautiful horns. At one time there were thousands of oryx living in the Arabian peninsula. Then, forty years ago, poachers began to use guns and trucks to hunt the oryx. They chased them until they dropped from exhaustion and then shot them. By the 1950s, the number of oryx had dropped from the thousands to less than one hundred. The last wild animal was seen in 1972. After that, the only oryx left were in zoos.

But luckily that wasn't the end of the story. In 1962, people who wanted to save the oryx had captured three wild animals and sent them to the Phoenix Zoo in Arizona. The oryx in Arizona were bred with oryx from other zoos around the world. In 1982, ten animals were taken back to the country of Oman. They were to be looked after by the Harasis people.

By the early 1990s, there were one hundred Arabian oryx in the wild, most of them young animals that had been born there. By the end of the century, the Harasis expect there will be about three hundred Arabian oryx in their homeland.

THE DOLPHIN

by Mary Ann Coleman

glides through the glass
green waters of the Seaquarium,
remembering the deep calls
of whales,
the way he rolled
in great blue passages
of open sea
thinking out loud.
Song-thought.
Shrill notes as he rose
through plankton and sea-weed,
gleams of the sun that drifted
    down
        down
covering his skin
with golden nets.

Evening. He lifts
from the tank,
jumping free.
Sees the moon,
splintering its silver
against the waves.

Afterward his clicks,
chitters, whistles
become a longing,
his speech a song
that includes the moon,
its glitter in an ocean
blue as the long-ago sea
calling inside him.

Listening,
he waits for an answer.

ACTIVITY

Do Zoos Help Save Wildlife?

How exactly do zoos help save wildlife? One way is to allow scientists to study the animals to see if they can learn how to save them in the wild. Another way is to keep alive animals that have been completely wiped out in their natural habitats. Zoos also breed some endangered animals, and hatch eggs taken from nests of **rare** birds. The young birds are raised and later released in their natural homes.

Find out whether a zoo or aquarium you know about is trying to save endangered species. You could:

- visit it and find out which of its animals are endangered
- write to it for information about saving endangered animals and whether it breeds any endangered animals
- invite someone from it to talk to your class about how they care for endangered animals. Ask whether there

are plans to release any of the animals in their natural habitats.

When you have enough information, make a display that answers the question "Do zoos help save wildlife?" You may want to divide your display into two parts, one in favor of zoos and one against.

Little Orphan Ape

Story and photos by Evelyn Gallardo

This sad-eyed young orangutan now lives wild and free. Would she remember the man who had been her "mother" three years before?

It was hot. Scorching hot. Stifling hot. Steamy jungle hot. It was July in Borneo (a big island north of Australia). And it could get much hotter. But my friend David Root and I didn't really care.

We had just volunteered to spend the next three weeks working for a famous scientist. Her name is Dr. Biruté Galdikas (BEER-oo-TAY GOLL-duh-kus). She studies wild orangutans (ooo-RANG-ooo-tahns). And she knows more about these great red apes than anyone else alive.

We were on board a boat with Dr. Galdikas, motoring upriver towards her camp. I watched a big-nosed monkey in a vine-wrapped tree shake a branch at us as we passed. But David had eyes only for the pitiful creature cradled in his arms. It was a three-year-old orphaned orangutan.

Her mother had been shot, and the infant had been sold as a pet. (This is against the law, but it still

happens.) When the "good guys" caught up with the people who had bought this baby, they rescued her at once. But she had probably spent a year or more with poor care and poor food. She had become sick and weak. So now we were taking her upriver with us for help.

We knew that when we got to camp, this young ape's life would get better. There she would find other orphans like herself. All were there to get "jungle survival training," which would help them return to the wild. But until she was stronger, she was going to need extra help. That's where David and I fitted in. He would be this infant's "coach." And I would take photographs and keep records of what went on.

MOVING IN

It took us six hours to reach the camp. At the dock, Dr. Galdikas hopped ashore and took the little orphan ape in her arms. "The first thing we have to do is give you a name," she said. She chose

"Davida," in honor of David. He was so pleased you could have lit up the sky with his smile.

Next, we took a look around. Our new home was in one of the eight buildings making up the camp. Surrounding us was a maze of tree-lined trails, with rivers, swamps, and forests beyond.

Because the orphaned orangutans move freely about camp, there are two important rules: Keep your doors locked, and watch out for the Dirty Tricks Gang.

The "gang" was made up of three young apes named Siswi, Supinah, and Rombe. While the other orphans practised tree-climbing and food-finding in the forest, *these* three hung around camp. They practised sneaker-snatching, cabin-raiding, and hitching rides on human "taxis."

One day David forgot to lock the door to our cabin. We had to get his shoes back from the orangutan gang with bribes of ripe bananas.

Another time his soap was stolen while he bathed in the lagoon (a shallow pond). The "thief" lathered her arm, then licked off the bubbles as if they were whipped cream!

MOVING UP

Day by day, Davida got better. At the end of only one week, we could see a difference. David spent hours bathing her, brushing her, and spoon-feeding her. He carried her everywhere, as her own mother would have done.

When David tried to put Davida down, she screeched and pounded her fists. She calmed down only when he wrapped her in his arms, giving her big, comforting hugs.

One day we had to leave Davida alone in the cabin for a very short while. We hoped she would be fine,

and she was. But we had a surprise waiting for us when we got home. There sat Davida on a "nest" of spilled vitamins, scattered clothing, squeezed-out tubes, and empty bottles. Boy, had she had fun!

"If you're strong enough to make such a mess," we decided, "you're

This forest business was scary! David had to climb into the tree with her until she felt safe enough to sit alone.

David also showed Davida how to build leafy nests on low branches. In these she would sit and rest. Some day she would build her own nests higher up in the trees.

MOVING ON

By the end of our second week, Davida was starting to swing from branches. She also began tasting fruit, leaves, and bark—but only after David had tasted them first. Was she ready to be with the other young orphans?

The apes were fed twice each day at a place called the "feeding bridge." They went there for ripe fruit, rice, and milk until they were able to find "wild" food in the forest. Knowing that Davida was hungry, David took her along at feeding-time.

He ran into trouble right away. When David sat Davida down next

to the other apes, she got very upset. She shrieked and leaped back into his arms. The other apes, however, wanted to be friendly.

▲ **"Up you go," urges David as an infant orangutan tackles its first tree. Davida was afraid at first too. Now she's a pro.**

well enough for your first trip into the forest." So the next day, off we went.

The forest seemed still and quiet as Davida moved timidly into a tree. But suddenly a flying squirrel *whizzed* overhead. Davida leaped back frantically into David's arms.

Several of the young orphans tried to touch little Davida. They only wanted to "adopt" her by pulling her on to their backs. But Davida wanted nothing to do with them. She cried and rejected each one with a painful bite. They were willing to accept *her* as one of them. But she wouldn't accept *them*. She had been captured too young to remember her own kind.

MOVING OUT

The weeks had sped past, and now our time in Borneo was almost up. But there was still so much for Davida to learn. Orangutans stay with their mothers for around seven years. Davida, however, had no mother and was afraid of the other orangutans. Who would teach her what she needed to know to survive?

David was really broken up about leaving. He even said he would quit his job if he could stay and help Davida. But Dr. Galdikas told us that everything would probably be fine. We had helped Davida when she needed it most. Now she could make it without the extra help. We had to trust that she would. But we couldn't help worrying about her.

◀ **An older orphan ape begs for food. But Davida gets fed first. Soon David will leave, but Davida will be OK. Her home is now the forest.**

THE RETURN

Three years went by before David and I could get back to Borneo. Would our small red friend remember us?

We arrived just at feeding-time. Several orangutans were gathered at the feeding bridge, and Davida was among them! She had tripled in size and looked much older. But it was Davida—without a doubt!

David offered her a stalk of sugar cane, which she took. But she turned her back on him each time he reached for her. She *didn't* remember.

"Of course she does," said Dr. Galdikas, later. "But she's punishing you, David. You were her 'parent,' and you abandoned her, at least from her point of view." David was sad, but he understood.

For the next couple of days, David kept trying to make friends with Davida. But she really seemed to have changed and would have little to do with him.

Finally, after a few days, Davida joined us on the porch. She stared at David a long while. Then she crawled up into his lap and touched his cheek. She was ready to "make up."

After that, Davida nested in a tree near David's room. We were there for a month, and she stayed nearby every night. This was really unusual. Orangutans usually build a new nest in a different tree each night.

We learned that Davida had never accepted another person the way she had David. She had never

▲ **This infant orangutan rests in its nest.**

accepted an orangutan as a substitute mother, either. Instead she had twice disappeared into the forest. Each time she had been gone for months. Each time her companion was an orangutan that had been captive for only a short

time. And each time she came back alone.

But it seemed that Davida had learned a lot. Now she appeared very comfortable in the trees. She knew which fruit and leaves to eat. She hung upside down and swatted gently at David as if he were another ape. She dug for grubs and lopped off tops of termite mounds to get at the insects inside. She seemed healthy and content in her forest home.

GOODBYE AGAIN

It rained the day David and I left again. Davida wasn't there. She had gone off into the forest, probably to find shelter. David never got the chance to tell her goodbye.

As our boat pulled away, he scanned the trees one last time. David was once again sad to go. But he was very glad at how things had turned out. He had helped return a little orphan ape to the wild. He thinks it is the most important thing he has ever done.

Meet Dr. Galdikas!

by Sallie Luther

Motoring down a jungle river with a crew of kids and apes—it's all in a day's work for this world-famous scientist.

"Wading all day up to my armpits in black swamp water wasn't too bad," says Dr. Biruté Galdikas. "It was those leeches! They would crawl under our clothing, hide in our socks, and even fall out of our underwear!"

She is talking about the early days of her work with wild orangutans. In 1971, she had come to the thick, steamy rainforests of Borneo. She and her husband lived in a bark hut, and their closest neighbors were six hours away by river boat.

Now, over twenty years later, her camp is a "neighborhood" itself. It is filled and busy with students, scientists—and dozens of orphaned orangutans. Dr. Galdikas is now the world's leading expert on the red apes.

To study a wild orangutan, Dr. Galdikas follows it all day, every day, for as long as it takes to get close. "After a while it gets used to you," she says, "and it doesn't even seem to care that you're there." Once a minute, she writes down what the ape is doing. These facts give an idea of an orangutan's way of life.

Dr. Galdikas now has three children. "My oldest son, Binti Paul, had only orphaned orangutans as playmates for a while," she remembers. "He could do a perfect imitation of one. In fact," she adds, "we had to keep a close eye on Bin. He would try to follow the orphans into trees!"

Working with the orphaned orangutans is very important to Dr. Galdikas. She and her staff return every one they can to the wild. Orangutans, like their gorilla and chimpanzee cousins, are becoming quite rare. Each one she saves helps keep the apes that much safer from disappearing forever.

THE CALL OF THE CRANES

Whooping cranes, the biggest birds in North America, stand 1 1/2 metres tall and have a wingspread of two metres. Their feathers are snowy white with black markings, and they have a patch of bright red skin on the tops of their heads. Whoopers used to live in marshlands across eastern and central North America. But hunters shot many of them, and farmers and settlers drained the marshlands they depended on. By 1941, there were only fifteen left.

A wildlife refuge was created in Texas, where the whooping cranes wintered every year. But no one knew where the whoopers nested and raised their young. Then, in 1954, a pilot in northern Canada discovered their nesting sites. Whoopers were migrating nearly four thousand kilometres from their winter home in Texas to their summer home in the Northwest Territories!

Scientists knew that whooping cranes lay two eggs each season, but that only one of the young cranes usually survives. They decided to remove one egg from each nest and hatch it at a scientific research station. The captive whoopers would be bred, or released in the wild.

Today, whooping cranes are still on the endangered list. But now there are more than 150 of them in North America. With luck, the wonderful whoopers will survive.

A CTIVITY

Saving Endangered Wildlife

Is there anything you can do to help save endangered wildlife? Here's how kids from Saskatchewan and New York State took action.

FLYING HIGH

You don't have to travel to South America to help peregrine falcons. Sarah and Stéphane Bonneville, Lina Chakrabarty, Odelia Chan, and Sonya Yong began at home by asking their families

for help. The group also held a bake sale at school and Stéphane made a speech about peregrines in every class. The money they raised went to the Saskatchewan Co-operative Falcon Project.

Sarah was surprised that few people knew about the peregrines. But thanks to her group, now more people know!

HOOT CLUB AWARD WINNERS

SMALL HANDS, BIG HELP

How is an almost weightless Karner blue butterfly like a 130-tonne blue whale? "They're both in danger of becoming extinct," says Kim Beil, 8. There's little Kim can do directly to rescue the whales. But, with four classmates from Lynnwood Elementary School in Guilderland, New York, she's doing plenty for the butterflies.

The larvae, or young, of the Karner blue eat only one kind of plant, the wild blue lupine. Lupines are vanishing as developers clear land for houses and shopping malls. With them go the butterflies.

Kim and her classmates collect lupine seedpods at a butterfly preserve for later planting at state-selected sites. In one morning they gathered some nine thousand seeds. They hope their efforts will generate new colonies of Karner blues.

Local projects like this are a good way to get involved in the fight to save endangered species. Work with some friends to decide how *you* could take action. What did the kids in the articles do? Which of the steps below would come first?

- Learning More about the Problem
- Taking Action
- Getting Publicity
- Working with Others
- Identifying a Wildlife Problem

Now choose an endangered species that you want to help save. Where will you start? What will you have to do? Decide where to begin, and then divide the work among the group. Keep a record of your progress!

WHAT <u>YOU</u> CAN DO

Find out how to turn your backyard or school grounds into a wildlife habitat.

Write to your state or provincial wildlife office to find out what wildlife species in your area are rare or endangered. Ask what you can do to help them survive.

Check out library books on endangered species to learn more about problems they face and what is being done to solve them.

Plan an endangered wildlife bike-a-thon or walk-a-thon. Ask sponsors to pledge money for each kilometre that is covered. Send the money you earn to an organization that's helping to save endangered species.

Join a group in your community that is working to save endangered plants and animals.

Volunteer to work at a zoo, park, or refuge near your home. Find out if your class can adopt a plant or animal there.

Products made from endangered animals.

Show you care by not buying a wild animal as a pet, or any items that are made from parts of endangered animals.

Work with some friends to put on an endangered wildlife display at a library or shopping mall.

A FLOCK OF ACTIVITIES

Find a song about endangered animals. Play or sing it for the class.

How can a shrub save a whale? (HINT: Jojoba)

Become a wildlife watcher. Tell a friend about something "wild" you have seen.

What is the difference between a reserve and a sanctuary?

Find out about the alligator comeback. You could draw a cartoon to show what you learned.

Do rhinoceroses have a right to exist? Do baboons? Do periwinkles?

Name three plants that are important for medicines.

Write a poem about an endangered animal. Tell how you feel about this animal.

What do you lose when an animal or plant becomes extinct?

Tell someone why wildlife is important to you.

ENDANGERED WILDLIFE WORD LIST

conservationist	A person who works to protect wildlife
domesticated	Depending on humans for food, shelter, and breeding
endangered wildlife	Species close to becoming extinct
extinct	No longer in existence
habitat	Natural home of a plant or animal
native	Belonging naturally to a certain place
rare	Seldom seen or found
species	All living things of the same kind that can breed together
threatened wildlife	Species that may soon become endangered
transplant	Plant again in a different place
tropical rainforests	Forests that grow near the equator where the climate is warm and wet all year round
vulnerable wildlife	Species at risk because of their small numbers
wildlife refuge	An area where wildlife is protected